AF323373

# DEEPWATER SHARKS

# DEEPWATER SHARKS

By Joyce A. Hull

MASON CREST

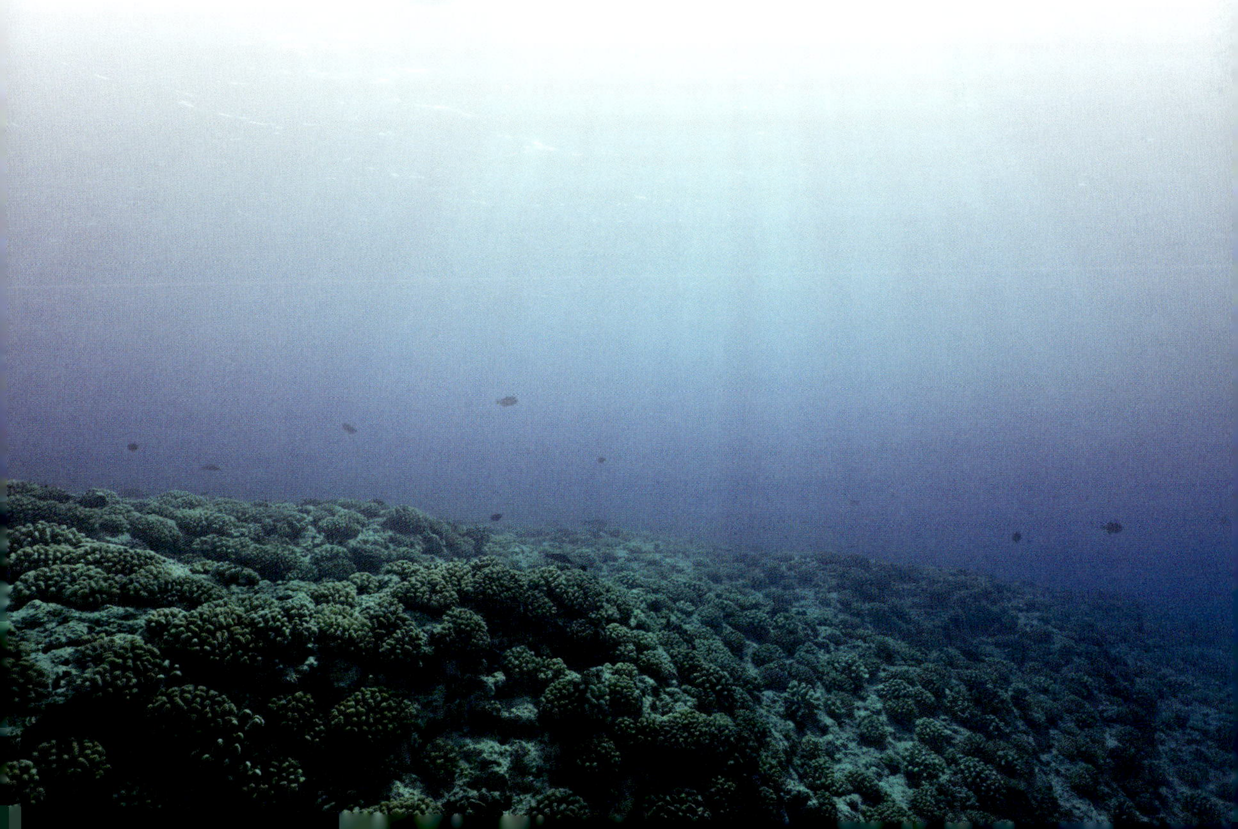

Mason Crest
450 Parkway Drive, Suite D
Broomall, Pennsylvania 19008
(866) MCP-BOOK (toll-free)
www.masoncrest.com



First printing
9 8 7 6 5 4 3 2 1
Printed in the USA

ISBN (hardback) 978-1-4222-4124-0
ISBN (series) 978-1-4222-4121-9
ISBN (ebook) 978-1-4222-7673-0

Library of Congress Cataloging-in-Publication Data

Names: Hull, Joyce A., author.
Title: Deepwater sharks / Joyce A. Hull.
Description: Broomall, Pennsylvania: Mason Crest, [2019] | Series: The  amazing world of sharks | Includes bibliographical references and index.
Identifiers: LCCN 2018013887 (print) | LCCN 2018018837 (ebook) | ISBN 9781422276730 (eBook) | ISBN 9781422241240 (hardback) | ISBN 9781422241219 (series)
Subjects: LCSH: Sharks--Juvenile literature. | Ocean bottom--Juvenile literature. | Deep diving--Juvenile literature.
Classification: LCC QL638.9 (ebook) | LCC QL638.9 .H85 2019 (print) | DDC 597.3--dc23
LC record available at https://lccn.loc.gov/2018013887

Developed and Produced by National Highlights Inc.
Editor: Keri De Deo and Mika Jin
Interior and cover design: Priceless Digital Media
Production: Michelle Luke

## QR CODES AND LINKS TO THIRD-PARTY CONTENT

# CONTENTS



## KEY ICONS TO LOOK FOR:

**Words to Understand:** These words with their easy-to-understand definitions will increase the reader's understanding of the text while building vocabulary skills.

**Sidebars:** This boxed material within the main text allows readers to build knowledge, gain insights, explore possibilities, and broaden their perspectives by weaving together additional information to provide realistic and holistic perspectives.

**Educational Videos:** Readers can view videos by scanning our QR codes, providing them with additional educational content to supplement the text. Examples include news coverage, moments in history, speeches, iconic sports moments, and much more!

**Text-Dependent Questions:** These questions send the reader back to the text for more careful attention to the evidence presented there.

**Research Projects:** Readers are pointed toward areas of further inquiry connected to each chapter. Suggestions are provided for projects that encourage deeper research and analysis.

**Series Glossary of Key Terms:** This back-of-the book glossary contains terminology used throughout this series. Words found here increase the reader's ability to read and comprehend higher-level books and articles in this field.

# FUN FACTS...
# GETTING TO KNOW THEM

### TIGER SHARK

Named for the vertical striped markings along its body, but they fade with age.

### MAKO SHARK

Known as the race car of sharks for its fast swimming speed!

### BULL SHARK

Named for its stocky shape, broad, flat snout, and aggressive, unpredictable behavior!

### RAYS

Rays and sharks belong to the same family. A ray is basically a flattened shark.

GREAT WHITE SHARK
With jaws this fierce, they don't call it "Great" for nothing!

BLUE SHARK
Known by their distinct blue and white coloring, their large eyes, and long snout.

HAMMERHEAD SHARK
Yes, those are eyes mounted on the side of its head, giving it 360-degree vision!

THRESHER SHARK
This clever shark uses its unique long tail fin to stun and catch prey!

## WORDS TO UNDERSTAND:

**filter feeder:** An animal that gets its food by filtering tiny animal and plant particles from water it takes in, usually through its mouth.
**oceanographer:** A scientist who studies all parts of the ocean, from how the water behaves to sea life and volcanoes.
**plankton:** Tiny sea animals that float with the current and provide an essential food source to many sea creatures.
**trench:** A long, narrow ditch, which is often the deepest part of the ocean.

### CHAPTER 1

# INTRODUCING DEEPWATER SHARKS

How far down in the ocean does a shark have to live to be considered a deepwater shark? **Oceanographers** generally agree that any area below 984 ft. (300 m) is considered deepwater. To put this in perspective, the Eiffel Tower is exactly this height. Imagine how much water it would take to completely cover the Eiffel Tower. Another way to imagine this depth is to think about the tall buildings in your town. Normally one story is equal to 10 ft. (3 m). Imagine a building that is ninety-eight stories high! This is the beginning of the deep water. So far, the deepest part of the ocean that has been found is the

Imagine how much water it would take to cover the Eiffel Tower!

Mariana **Trench**. It goes down 7 mi. (11.27 km) from the ocean surface. There are sharks that live at that extreme depth! We will be learning more about these sharks later in this book.

*This video describes fourteen of the most unusual sharks that have been discovered so far.*

The deep ocean holds many mysteries, such as this six-gilled shark.

## THE SHARK AND THE OCTOPUS

Most cultures pass down myths and legends for centuries. Many of these stories were created to explain things that people do not know or understand. Others were created to help teach lessons to others. Today, children on the island of Fiji are taught a story that helps them feel less afraid of sharks. It is not known how long ago this story started, but it is highly possible that Fijian children are hearing the same story their grandparents and great-grandparents heard when they were young.

According to the Fijian legend, in the days when gods ruled the world, a god named Takuaka controlled one of the many reefs in the area. Takuaka took the form of a shark and he became jealous of all the other reef gods, so he would fight with each one to take control of his or her reef. During many of the fights, the ocean waves became high and the people on the islands feared that they would drown. But Takuaka always prevailed. After he had beaten all the reef protectors in his area, he heard of one last guardian who took the form of a large octopus. Takuaka saw how large the octopus was but tried his best to beat it. The octopus held onto the reef with four of its tentacles and wrapped the other four around the jealous god, squeezing so hard that Takuaka found it difficult to breathe, and the reef god thought he was going to die.

Being a gentle creature at heart, the octopus agreed that he would not kill Takuaka if the shark agreed to never again bother the people on the reefs. Takuaka knew he had to make this promise and has kept it to this today. That is why sharks and the island people live in harmony.

## MYSTERIES

In extremely deep water, there is a lot of pressure that makes it difficult for humans to survive. Even with breathing gear, the pressure is so strong that the human body can be crushed. That is why these deep waters hold so many mysteries. A few people have been able to go to the bottom of the ocean for a short period of time in special submarines, but they have not been able to stay long enough to get a thorough idea of everything that lives down there. Most of what we know has been discovered by specialized cameras designed to withstand the pressure. We now have submarines that can stay on the ocean floor for a few hours and are capable of tagging some species of sharks. All of these things help us learn more about the mysteries hiding in the ocean depths.

Water becomes colder the deeper it gets. It also becomes darker because the sun's rays do not penetrate the water so far down. Oceanographers need to find ways to account for both the cold and the darkness, which makes it difficult to study the deep ocean. Sharks that live in these deep waters have developed many ways to make it possible to survive. This is why the sharks that we have discovered in the deep ocean often look different than the ones we see in shallow waters. A new type of shark is discovered every few years, but it is possible that we have not discovered many of the inhabitants of these waters. Considering that we have yet to explore nearly 95 percent of the oceans, there are many mysteries to be discovered. Scientists believe that we know more about outer space than we know about what lives in the water on our own planet!

This dwarf lantern shark is one of the smallest sharks found in the deep ocean.

Many plankton, such as these copepoda zooplankton, can only be seen with a microscope.



### BIG AND DANGEROUS—NOT!

We know very little about the deepest parts of the ocean, which makes many humans think that anything living that far down has to be both big and dangerous, but this is not the case. The biggest shark, the whale shark, lives in the deep water, yet this shark eats mainly **plankton**. It does sometimes eat fish, but it is mainly a **filter-feeding** shark. On the other hand, the smallest shark, the dwarf lanternfish also lives in deep water. This shark grows to only 7½ in. (19 cm). The dwarf lanternfish prefers the deepwater because it is easier for it to hide from prey. While there are many deepwater sharks that can be seen as dangerous, humans rarely come into contact with them because we do not spend much time in these deep waters. Sharks, in general, will not attack unless they feel threatened. Even when they do bite a human, most sharks will quickly realize their mistake and let go.

## TIME TO EXPLORE

As you continue through this reading adventure, you will discover some of the most unusual sharks in the entire world. Some we have learned a lot about, but others we still know very little about. Going into the deep water is like visiting a country that is thousands of miles away. Things may look different and behavior may vary. After all, people living in a hot desert live life very differently than those living in the Arctic Circle. Yet, just as people are people, the sharks that live in the deepest parts of the ocean are still sharks. Some are small, others large, most eat meat, and still others eat plankton. In the end, however, each is as unique and wonderful as all the others. Maybe one day you will find your way to the ocean floor and discover a new kind of shark that nobody else has yet seen. Wouldn't that be exciting?

The frilled shark is a newly discovered deepwater shark species.

## TEXT-DEPENDENT QUESTIONS:

1. How deep is the Mariana Trench?

2. What kind of shark may make humans think they saw a sea serpent and why?

3. What special conditions in deep ocean water make it necessary for the sharks that live there to have characteristics that are different from their shallow-water relatives?

## RESEARCH PROJECT:

Before James Cameron dove down 7 mi. (11.3 km) to the bottom of the Mariana Trench, there were two others who did the same. Who were these men, and what was their story? How did the two trips to the same spot differ? Do you think anyone else will be able to stay on the bottom longer in the future? Why or why not?

WORDS TO UNDERSTAND:

**adapt:** The process of an animal changing to survive in its environment.

**bioluminescence:** The result of a chemical reaction in some animals that allows them to produce and give off light, essentially allowing them to glow in the dark. This type of glowing animal is able to be seen by humans.

**electroreception:** A shark's ability to detect electrical impulses given off by living things.

# DEEPWATER SHARKS' POPULATION AND HABITAT

Dark and cold are the two words that best describe the deep waters of our oceans. The environment that deepwater sharks inhabit makes it difficult to use only their eyes for hunting. Their body temperatures have to adjust to colder waters, and they have to find ways to survive in the higher pressure that exists at the bottom of the ocean. The sharks that live in the deepest water each have found unique ways to **adapt**. Some of these ways are easily seen, while others are more difficult to learn about because they are inside the shark's body. In both cases, however, these changes are crucial for the survival of ocean life.

Deepwater sharks, like this whale shark, have learned how to adapt in a cold, dark environment.

## ENHANCED SENSES

Many deepwater sharks have heightened senses of smell and larger eyes that allow them to see better in the dark. They also have a special sense called **electroreception**. All of these things work together to allow the sharks to find prey more easily. Their diets often consist of the same kinds of prey that shallow water sharks enjoy, such as fish, crustaceans, and mollusks. However, the variety available to them is different because it is not only the sharks that must adapt to the deeper waters, but all the plants and animals too. The sharks also need to develop ways to live with less oxygen and move in water that is higher in pressure than in shallower water.

This rare image of a Greenland shark shows its size.

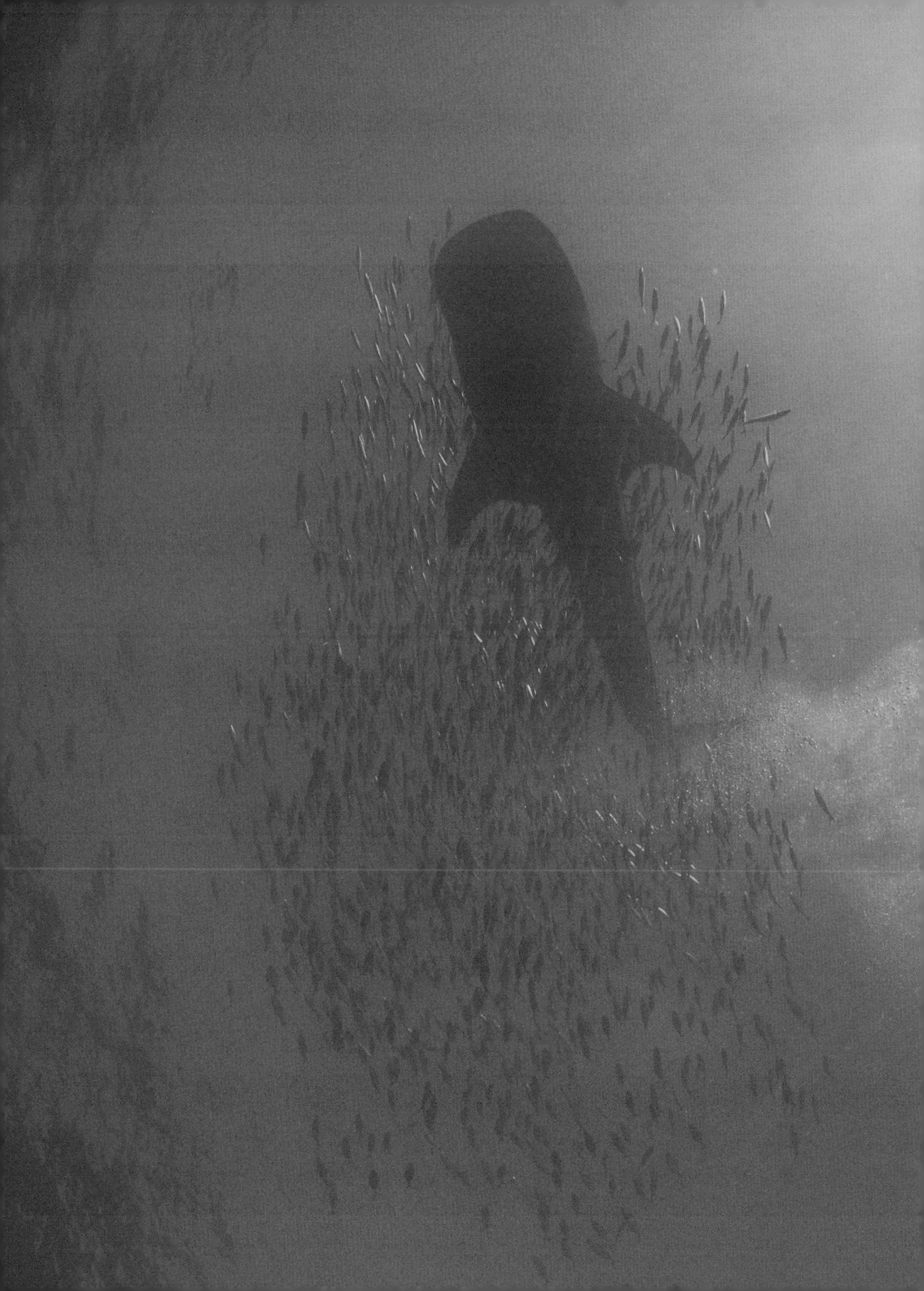

# SLOWER AND MORE BUOYANT

Sharks that inhabit the deeper waters are often slower moving. The Greenland sleeper shark is one example. This large shark only moves at about 1 mph (1.6 kph). When you compare this to the short-finned mako, which travels at more than 35 mph (56 kph), it is a big difference. This slower movement is not caused by size but by the pressure that the surrounding water exerts on their bodies. Several deepwater sharks find it easier to simply float whenever possible. Floating also allows them to reserve more energy for regulating body temperature.

Another adaptation that deepwater sharks have is in their livers. A shark gets its ability to stay afloat by the amount of oil present in its liver. The deeper a shark lives, the larger its liver is in comparison to the rest of its body. This is because the liver contains more oil, allowing the shark to be able to stay afloat and not sink to the bottom of the ocean or rise too close to the surface. This increased amount of oil in their livers is intended to help the sharks, but it is one of the main reasons they are in danger from fishermen. The oil is used to make things like cosmetics and even some medications, and deepwater fishermen catch these sharks solely for their livers. This overfishing of deepwater sharks may put some of them in danger before we have a chance to learn more about them.

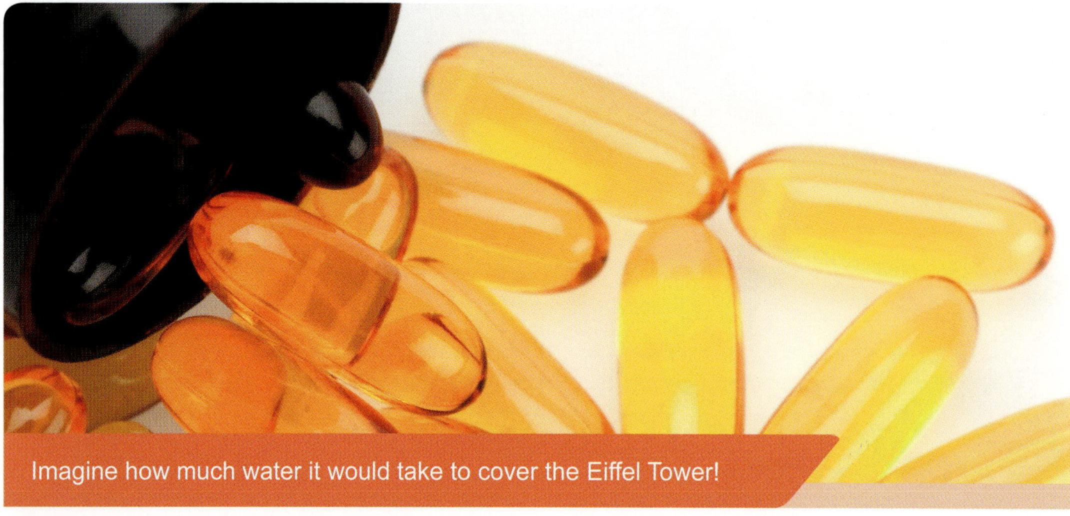
Imagine how much water it would take to cover the Eiffel Tower!

## LIGHTING UP THE SEA

Some sharks are **bioluminescent**. In essence, these sharks glow in the dark. This glowing is thought to be used as a means of communicating, finding a mate, locating food, and providing camouflage. Exactly how the bioluminescence is used is as varied as the number of creatures that can do it—over fifty different species! For instance, lantern sharks use it to help them identify other members of the same species. It is thought that the glowing lights might even indicate members of the opposite sex to help during mating. Scientists believe that each species of shark that carries this ability does it differently so other species are able to identify which kind of shark they are seeing and know whether they need to hide, hunt, or go about their business.

Bioluminescent organisms like these plankton glow in the dark under special lighting.

Most of the sharks that exhibit bioluminescence only do so on their bottom sides. **Marine biologists** do not know for sure, but they believe this helps the shark avoid detection by other animals. The glowing bellies eliminate any shadow produced by the shark, which is called counterillumination. Without the shadow, predators don't realize that the shark is near. It also keeps the shark's prey from knowing it is nearby. In this way, the glowing shark is able to sneak up on its prey, and avoid becoming prey to another animal.

The cookiecutter shark leaves distinctive bites on its prey.

The cookiecutter shark is one species that shows this bioluminescence over its entire body. Nobody knows why, but it could serve many different purposes. The cookiecutter is one of the smallest sharks in the deep water. It is possible that the entire body glowing helps it attract prey that is fascinated with the light. When the prey gets near enough, the small shark attacks. This shark got its name for its very strange way of eating, which we'll learn more about in chapter three!

**WHICH CAME FIRST?**

You have probably heard the question about whether the chicken or the egg came first. Scientists have often wondered the same thing about whether earth once held more water or more land. While this question has not been completely answered, the kind of sharks found in deep water can help provide clues to the answer. Those that have been discovered in the deepest waters have many of the same traits as their ancestors. The oldest sharks, and those with traits resembling the first sharks, live in the deepest recesses of the ocean. This tells scientists that it is highly possible that the oceans once covered more area than they do now, and that it is the shallow water sharks that have had to do the most adapting in order to survive. Can you think of other clues scientists have found that show water may have covered more of the earth in the distant past?

## DAY TRAVELERS

Some of the deepwater sharks stay near the bottom of the ocean during the night but will travel into shallower water during the day. This is called vertical migration, and they do it in order to increase the amount of food available to them. This means that the shark has to be able to adjust its body temperature somewhat in order to withstand the warmer temperatures in more shallow water. How this is done by most sharks is not yet known, but the great white shark may hold the answer.

The great white has what is called the rete mirabile, or wonderful net, near its gills. This network of arteries and veins warms the blood as water passes over the gills, allowing the great white to raise its body temperature a full ten degrees without causing any problems. It is possible that other deepwater sharks have this same ability, but scientists don't know enough about them in order to say this is how they survive. Ten degrees may not seem like a lot, but it is like a human being having a temperature of 108.6°F (43.6°C) instead of the normal 98.6°F (37°C). Unlike a human, however, this increase in temperature actually helps the shark instead of making it ill.

The main reason sharks go from deep water to shallower water is that they are searching for food. Another reason is to avoid the hunting times of predators. It is also possible that some sharks find the different views in the shallower water something interesting to explore. Finally, many sharks travel to shallow water to give birth. When baby sharks are born, they are too small to survive in the deepest waters, and mother sharks will often give birth in shallow water to give their pups the greatest chance of survival. Sharks tend to grow continually throughout their lives, and as the pups get older and bigger, they can find food at deeper levels. Occasionally, an injured or ill shark will be unable to stay afloat at the deeper levels and will end up in more shallow water. This is not intentional. In time, scientists may discover other reasons, but for now, these are the main reasons you may see deepwater sharks near a beach or in other shallow water.

Some deepwater sharks, like this whale shark, will come to the surface for food.

## UNUSUAL TRAITS

Some deepwater sharks have developed unusual characteristics that seem to have no explanation. Sometimes these traits are seen in only a few species of shark, and it is unclear why more species don't have the same traits. Knowing as little as we do about so many of the deepwater sharks, these are questions that will hopefully be answered in the future. Let's look at some of these special traits and what scientists think may be the reason for them.

The goblin shark is pink; the color is not bright, but more like a slight tint. This is because its blood vessels are very close to the surface of its skin and they break easily, causing bruising. Scientists don't know why this happens. So far, this is the only shark that has been discovered that exhibits this characteristic.

Perhaps you can tell from this photo how the goblin shark got its name.

Sand tiger sharks normally give birth to two pups at a time, but it's what happens before birth that sets them apart. When a female sand tiger shark becomes pregnant she usually has six to eight embryos, which she carries in two different uteruses. Instead of living on the yolk of an egg before birth as other shark species do, the embryos become cannibals and eat the others within their uterus. This leaves only one pup in each uterus to be born. This could be the way the sand tiger shark ensures only the strongest of the species survives. It does not seem like this cannibalism continues after the pups are born, however, which is good, or we might see the species disappear.

Frilled sharks have several unusual characteristics. Instead of five gills, they have six. Scientists haven't determined if this extra gill serves a purpose or not. The sixth gill is located across their throats. Unlike other sharks, this species has maintained the same skeletal structure that the earliest sharks had. This has gained them the nickname "fossil sharks." These sharks resemble large eels, but do not have the electricity in them that eels possess. They do, however, find it much easier to hide in small crevices to catch prey and to hide from those who would hunt them.

### NO VOICE

The deep oceans are alive with sounds. You have probably heard recordings of whale songs. Many fish make sounds, and the ocean itself is full of many kinds of songs. Sharks, however, are silent inhabitants of the ocean. Not only do they have no organs to create sound, but their scales are also designed to be silent as they swim through the water. One shark, called the draughtsboard shark, can be found in New Zealand and is reported to be able to "bark." What actually occurs, however, is that the shark has the same ability that is present in puffer fish. When frightened, it fills with air in order to appear larger, and when the air is expelled, the sound resembles a bark. This is not, however, done as a way to communicate. It is more like when a human being burps after drinking something with a lot of bubbles in it, and the air needs to escape. Sharks are truly some of the most silent inhabitants of the oceans.

# DEEP SEA SHARK POPULATION

It is impossible for us to know the true population of sharks in deep water. New species are being discovered every year as science advances and enables humans to explore deeper than before. We do know that sharks live in every area of the world, from the warmest oceans to the coldest ones. We know that some sharks are more numerous than others.

Some of the deepest parts of the ocean have not yet been explored.

Deepwater fishermen have shown this by the numbers of some species they catch in their nets. With other species, only one member of the species may have been seen. Some of these have only appeared briefly on the footage from cameras. Scientists can be almost certain that there are more members of that species, but they have no way of knowing how many more without more research. Only time and scientific advancements will be able to tell.

What we do know is that life at the bottom of the ocean and life near the surface is similar in some ways, and vastly different in others. We know that plants and animals exist in the depths of the ocean, and they have the same needs as those that live in shallow water or on land. Deepwater sharks are like every other animal species on earth. They hunt and are hunted. They have babies and grow old. Some of the most beautiful sharks discovered make their homes in this dark, watery world, as do some of the strangest-looking sharks. In the next chapter, we will take a look at individual species to show the variety of life that has been discovered beneath the waves of our world's oceans. There is not enough room to talk about all the sharks that are known to exist in the deepest waters of the world, but maybe getting this sample will encourage you to search for more information on your own.

## TEXT-DEPENDENT QUESTIONS:

1. Do all deepwater sharks stay near the ocean floor? If not, why would they move closer to the ocean's surface?

2. Explain what bioluminescence means. In what ways does having this trait help the sharks that possess it?

3. Which shark is an unusual color and why?

## RESEARCH PROJECT:

Gather two large bowls, two sticks of equal size (these are to represent your sharks), and two plants or leaves of equal size and shape. Place one stick and one plant in each bowl. Now, fill the first bowl all the way to the top, making sure there are at least six inches of water in the bowl. In the second bowl, only put in an inch or two of water. Wait for three or four hours and check on the plants and sticks.

What do you see happening? Both the plants and sticks will react differently to the water level. This shows how objects will not always behave the same when water levels change. Now try placing a cotton ball in each dish. What happens to the cotton ball in the deep water? This shows why sharks that live in deep water need to develop different traits than those living in shallow water. Each shark needs special traits that help it survive in its chosen environment. Try making some changes, like putting a notch in one stick or reshaping the leaf. Does this make a difference in the results?

## WORDS TO UNDERSTAND:

**biofluorescence:** The ability of some animals to emit light by absorbing blue light and reflecting it back out, usually as red, orange, or green light. The glow produced by this type of animal is only visible to each other, or to humans using special equipment.
**gestation period:** The length of time a female is pregnant.
**planktivore:** A sea creature that feeds on plankton, which is small plants and animals.
**upwelling:** The movement of cold water from the depths of the ocean toward the surface.

### CHAPTER 3

# DEEPWATER SHARKS' DIET, BEHAVIOR, AND BIOLOGY

In this chapter, you will get a chance to meet some of the most interesting sharks that inhabit the deepest ocean water. A few of these were introduced earlier, but many will be new. Some we know a great deal about, and others are still pretty much a mystery. In all cases, they are fascinating! With all the unusual specimens that we know of, it is exciting to think about what other sharks we will find in the future.

## FRILLED SHARK

You met the frilled shark earlier. This shark got its name because the edge of each of its six gills has a red frill. Only one of these sharks has ever been captured alive, and it lived only a few hours, indicating that it may be impossible for the frilled shark to survive outside of its normal environment, which is 400 to 4200 ft. (121.92 to 12,892 m) below the surface of the ocean. It is possible this particular shark was already ill, but since no other member of the species has been caught, it is impossible to know for sure.

The frilled shark gets its name from its "frilly" gills.

It is often the case that sharks normally living in the deepest waters do not survive when captured. Even though they may seem scary to humans, a shark has a very delicate nervous system that sometimes becomes overloaded and stops working when it is captured. Since frilled sharks also have a delicate immune system, it is possible that we will never be able to see one survive in captivity.

Not only is the frilled shark's immune system extremely delicate, but so are its digestive system and other senses. This makes the frilled shark vulnerable to changes in environmental conditions. In addition, the frilled shark is unable to unhinge its jaw like other sharks, which makes it more difficult for it to catch certain prey. It feeds mainly on squid, fish, and smaller sharks. The shape of this unusual shark may be to blame for its weak immune system and senses, but that is something that needs to be studied in greater detail before a conclusion can be made.

The frilled shark is similar to an eel in shape. This gives it easier access to hiding places and allows it to enter crevices after prey. It is believed that the frilled shark strikes at prey in the same way a snake does. This shark can grow as long as 7 ft. (2.13 m) in length. If you can picture a long snake with sharp teeth, you have an idea of what this shark looks like.

The frilled shark is also the one that has the longest **gestation period**. The female carries her pups for a full three and a half years, and normally gives birth to a litter of six pups. This long gestation period and the small number of pups make marine biologists believe that the number of frilled sharks is lower than other species.

The frilled shark has especially white teeth. It is possible that the glow of the teeth attracts prey in the otherwise dark of the deep ocean. As prey nears to see what is glowing, the frilled shark strikes from its hiding place and captures its prey. This shark has three hundred teeth, and they are sharp and slanted slightly backward. This makes it impossible for any prey to escape the shark's mouth. Even if the shark barely catches its prey, the slant of the teeth helps the shark get a better grip that draws the prey inward.

The frilled shark's teeth slant inward to better hold its prey.

## SWELL SHARK

The swell shark lives 1,500 ft. (approximately 457 m) beneath the ocean's surface, and is an example of a **biofluorescent** animal. When humans look at these sharks they see a leopard-spotted shark. The swell shark has hundreds of spots that glow when seen by another shark, or a special camera made to see like a shark does.

This shark is thought to glow for two main reasons. The first is a way of communicating with other sharks of the same species. This helps let other members of the swell shark family feel safe and know they are not in danger. It also seems to send a message from a male or female shark that tells the other when it is time for mating.

The neon green swell shark only looks green under special lighting.

The second is a means of camouflage. Many of the plants and animals that inhabit the deepest parts of the ocean give off a slight glow. It is not known for sure why this is so, but scientists believe it is a way these plants and animals have learned to adapt to the darkness. The glow produced by the swell shark helps it blend in more completely.

Swell sharks are found in the Pacific Ocean. They got their name for an unusual habit they have when they feel threatened. When a swell shark feels scared, it swallows as much water as it can. This causes its belly to swell up and make it look much bigger than it really is. The swell shark hopes this will scare away any predators, or at least make the swell shark too big to be swallowed. The swell shark typically eats small bony fish and crustaceans, such as crab and lobster.

## COOKIECUTTER SHARK

The cookiecutter shark is another one you were introduced to earlier when we learned about bioluminescent sharks. (Remember, this type of animal makes light through a chemical reaction, and the light is visible to humans.) This shark is often found in the waters off the coast of Brazil, at depths of up to 12,000 ft. (3.7 km). The shark's belly glows and there is a fish-shaped streak near its throat. This dark fish shape against the glowing skin looks like a fish to other ocean inhabitants and draws them near in hopes of getting a tasty meal. But instead, that is when the cookiecutter makes a meal out of the unsuspecting investigator.

In fact, the cookiecutter has a very strange way of eating. It attaches itself to its prey using

This close-up of the cookiecutter shark shows its tiny, sharp teeth.

its lips and sharp, pointy teeth. The shark then turns in a circle, using its teeth to take a circular chunk out of its prey. This leaves behind a wound that looks like a cookiecutter was used, giving this shark its name. While this method of feeding is surely painful, the bites inflicted by the cookiecutter shark are rarely fatal. In fact, large fish, sharks, whales, and even marine mammals are often found with scars from the cookiecutter shark's unusual feeding habit.

Like other sharks, the cookiecutter loses its teeth, and they are replaced. The bottom teeth, however, come out as one unit, much like a set of false teeth, and the shark swallows the entire set. Most likely, this is a way to gain more calcium, but scientists do not know this for certain. Cookiecutters are small sharks. The males only grow to be 15.5 in. (39.37 cm), and the females grow up to 22 in. (55 cm). Their small size does not stop these brave sharks from making a meal out of pieces of larger creatures such as great white sharks, whales, and dolphins.

**OLDEST LIVING SHARK SPECIES**

The Greenland shark is a type of sleeper shark that grows to the size of the great white shark. Scientists have found members of this species that live to be anywhere from four hundred to five hundred years of age, which makes them the longest living of any of the known shark species. These sharks do not even reach breeding age until they are about 150 years old. Their habitat in the deep, cold ocean waters around Greenland keeps them free from natural predators, giving them a chance to live out long lives. The only time they come close to shore is when they follow upwellings in search of prey. It is the great age of the Greenland sleeper that had scientists mistake it for the prehistoric Megalodon when they first encountered it. It would be a miracle if a Megalodon did still exist, but that is not likely.

## GOBLIN SHARK

With its lumpy body and pinkish color, the goblin shark is one of the most unusual-looking shark species. The goblin shark enjoys life at approximately 4000 ft. (1219 m) below the ocean's surface, making it one of the deepest dwellers yet to be discovered. It is thought to be widely distributed throughout the world, and has been found near almost every continent. Goblin sharks can grow as long as 12 ft. (3.36 m) and weigh 460 lbs. (208.652 kg). The goblin shark got its name because it looks like the mythological goblins in Japanese folk tales.

Given that it lives in the darkest parts of the ocean and has tiny eyes, the goblin shark must rely on its electrical sensors in order to find food. Once it finds prey, its teeth actually come forward a bit from its mouth, giving it extra reach. The teeth are attached to the goblin shark's jaw by flaps of skin that are 3 in. (7.6 cm) long. This means that the teeth can extend a full three inches outside the goblin shark's jaw!

Can you guess which tooth is from a megalodon?
The round fossil is a fossilized shark vertebra.

## MEGALODON

The biggest known shark was the megalodon. Recently, scientists discovered what they believed to be a living megalodon, but it turned out it was a species of sleeper shark. The closest living relative of this shark is the great white, but even it does not compare to the size and strength of its ancestor, who had the ability to crush a human skull with one bite. That did not happen, however, as the megalodon lived in the time of dinosaurs and did not have any contact with people. What we know today about this magnificent creature comes from fossils that have been found. Check out the video in this chapter to learn more about the megalodon.

The Greenland shark is the oldest known shark.

# MEGAMOUTH SHARK

The megamouth shark has only recently been discovered, and there have been fewer than one hundred members of the species counted. This shark is one of only three **planktivores**, or filter-feeders. To eat, the megamouth swims with its mouth open, taking in both water and plankton. The water is then pushed out through the gills. What's special about the megamouth shark is that the inner lining of its gills are lined with finger-like projects that filter the plankton from the water as it passes out through the gills.

The megamouth shark was discovered in 1976 in an unusual manner. A Navy ship dropped two parachute anchors into deep water. When the anchors were brought up, a dead shark was found entangled in one of the anchors. This shark was over 14 ft. (4.2 m) long and looked like nothing anyone had ever seen before. It was amazing to marine biologists that such a large shark had never been seen before. It also made them question what other large inhabitants the oceans held. There have been so few megamouth sharks found that it is not known exactly where they call home. This is one mystery that still needs to be solved.

The skeleton of the megamouth is soft. This is a result of its limited diet. Normally the softer skeleton does not cause any issues. This slow-moving giant does not often have to worry about trying to escape predators because most other sea creatures are intimidated by its size. The one thing that is difficult for the megamouth is escaping fishing nets if it gets caught in one. It does not have the necessary strength to fight its way out of these nets. Unlike other sharks, the skin of the megamouth is loose and a bit saggy. This also causes a problem when the shark is caught, as it does not have the ability to slide free as easily as its smoother relatives do. In some ways, you can think of the megamouth shark as the ocean's version of an elephant. It is gentle, often slow-moving, and has saggy skin.

The megamouth belongs to a group of sharks called mackerel sharks. This group of sharks has remained basically unchanged for over thirteen hundred years. That means they are the closest relatives to ancient sharks. By learning about this group of sharks, scientists can get a better understanding

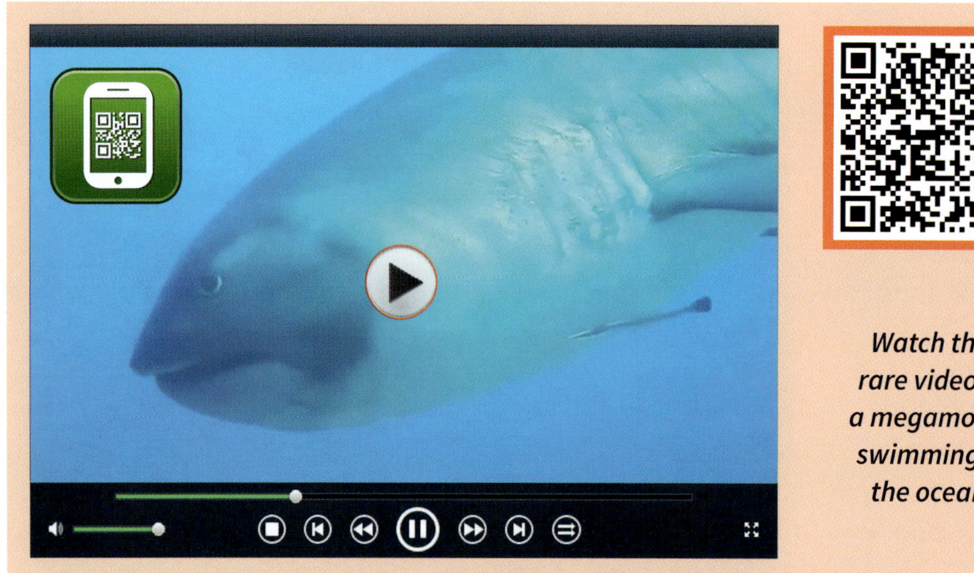

Watch this rare video of a megamouth swimming in the ocean.

of how ancient sharks evolved into their modern versions. The mackerel shark group includes such sharks as the great white, the shortfin mako, the salmon shark, the thresher shark, the sand tiger shark, the slow-moving basking shark, and the goblin shark. It is interesting to note that this slow-moving shark is related to one of the fastest sharks, the shortfin mako.

Another intriguing fact is that this group of sharks is warm-blooded. That means that they all have the ability to raise their body temperatures when necessary in order to survive in deep, cold water. Also of note is that even though they all belong to the same shark group, some live in warm water and others in icy oceans. Just like human cousins, this group of shark cousins is all different from each other.

In 2015, a marine biologist was able to tag a megamouth. This is a great achievement because it will enable us to learn more about this giant species, including where they like to live, how long their lifespan is, and many other interesting facts. So far, it has enabled scientists to learn of more megamouth sharks than they had previously discovered. The number is still low compared to most other species, but these sharks are not listed as endangered because we do not really know how many there are. It also has shown that these deepwater creatures sometimes come near the surface. This happens mostly during night hours and is a result of them following their favorite food. Megamouths love to eat krill and will follow schools of krill into the upper levels of the ocean in order to enjoy this meal.

The average depth of the ocean is about 12,100 ft. (3,688 m). The deepest part of the ocean, called the Challenger Deep, is located in the southern end of the Mariana Trench in the western Pacific Ocean. The Mariana Trench runs several hundred kilometers southwest of the U.S. territorial island of Guam. Challenger Deep is approximately 36,200 ft. (11,033.76 m) deep. It is named after the HMS *Challenger*, the first true oceanographic research vessel whose crew first discovered the depths of the trench in 1875.

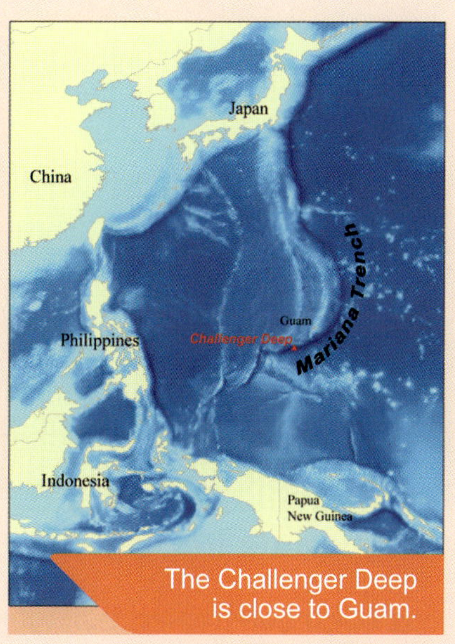


The Challenger Deep is close to Guam.

## PORTUGUESE DOGFISH

The Portuguese dogfish is another deepwater shark that we know very little about. These smallish sharks grow to be only about 5 ft. (1.5 m) in length. They are dark brown and have slender bodies and square-shaped fins. The Portuguese dogfish lives approximately 12,000 ft. (3657.6 meters) below the ocean's surface.

The upper teeth of the dogfish are pointy like spears, and the lower teeth are like blades. These sharks eat mainly octopus, squid, and small fish, although some have been observed eating the remains of kills made by other sea creatures. That is similar to what birds like seagulls and crows do. It is nature's way of making sure nothing goes to waste.

Portuguese dogfish are some of the deepest ocean dwellers. It is believed that they live for as long as seventy years. These sharks look a lot more like bony fish than other sharks. They lack some of the fins that most sharks have. The dogfish is part of the family of sharks called sleeper sharks because of their slow movements. This does not mean the dogfish is lazy, however. They are very stealthy hunters and will spend a great deal of time stalking their prey. Their slow movement can be beneficial when stalking. Their prey does not feel as alarmed by what appears to be a slow-floating shark that might even be sleeping. This allows the dogfish to get closer before its prey realizes it is about to be lunch.

This dogfish was found in the Sea of Japan.

It has been determined that the dogfish calls most of the Atlantic and some of both the Indian and Pacific Oceans home. Unlike many other species of sharks, the dogfish lives at different depths depending on its age and gender. Younger members of the species tend to live in deeper water. Pregnant females, however, prefer shallower water in which they can safely give birth. Males and females also live in different

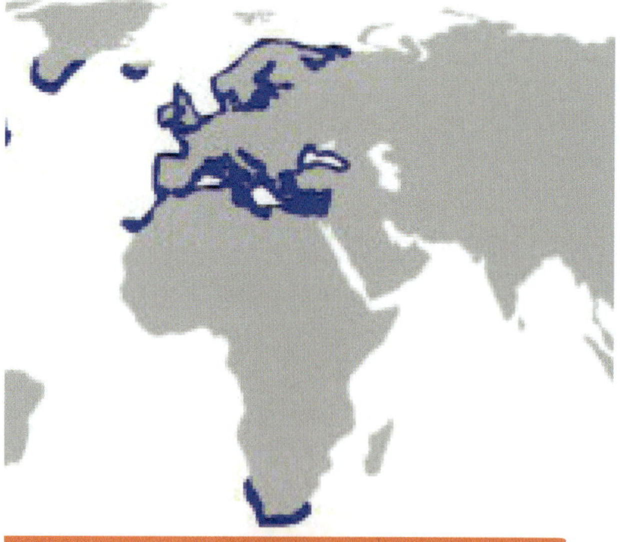
This map shows the estimated distribution of the spiny dogfish.

areas, except during mating times. It is not yet known why this occurs. So far, this seems to be the only known species of shark that has such a diverse living environment. Marine biologists do think the younger dogfish are safer in the deeper water. It is also thought that starting out in more shallow water and working their way to the deep water helps them gain strength and learn the skills necessary to survive into adulthood.

## MANY MORE

This is only a small sampling of the many deepwater sharks that inhabit our planet. With so much of the ocean yet to be explored, we are sure to discover many more. We know a lot about many of these sharks but very little about others. It may be hundreds of

There are so many more deepwater sharks than what's covered in this book, like this pyjama shark found in the deep waters by South Africa.

years before we learn all the secrets of these deepwater dwellers. Until then, we can only keep learning and exploring.

**TEXT-DEPENDENT QUESTIONS:**

1. How did the swell shark get its name?

2. What shark has the weakest immune system?

3. How long does the frilled shark carry her pups before they are born?

**RESEARCH PROJECT:**

Do some research on other biofluorescent and bioluminescent animals. Pick one from each group, and compare and contrast how each uses its glow. Write a two-page paper explaining the similarities and differences of those animals.

**WORDS TO UNDERSTAND:**

**marine biologists:** Scientists who study ocean life.

**oceanic:** Something related to the ocean.

**submersible:** Anything that can safely go under water.

**taxidermy:** Stuffing an animal that has died so that it still looks like it did when it was alive.

# ENCOUNTERING DEEPWATER SHARKS

Most deepwater sharks have never been seen in person by the average human. That means that these sharks have also never seen a human. What they have seen, however, are cameras, **submersibles**, and other exploration technology created to explore their world. Can you imagine what it would be like to be a shark swimming around and coming across

Submersibles like this mini submarine are used to capture deepwater shark images.

one of these items? It might try to taste whatever it finds, but most likely it will use its sensors to see if the item is alive. Finding that it isn't, the shark will lose interest and swim away. That is why deep-sea explorers have been able to get the videos they have. If you want to find out more about the sharks that live in the deep waters of our oceans, there are a few ways you can do this.

## WATCH VIDEOS

Explore some of the links that are in this book, and visit the websites of **oceanic** explorers like the *Okeanos Explorer* mentioned in the sidebar below. This awesome ship has explored many areas of the world's oceans. These scientists have been generous in sharing what they find beneath the water, and you can learn not only about the sharks but also about all the other plants and animals that are hiding beneath the waves. There is a whole other world under the ocean waiting to be discovered, and videos give us an amazing opportunity to see what's out there.

*This video shows a "forest" from the deep ocean floor that looks like something from another planet!*

Many of the deepwater sharks we have discovered have only been found when they washed up on beaches after they died, or they were caught in fishing nets. Those sharks that live in the deepest areas of the ocean can't survive in shallow water because they have adapted to the darker, colder water of the deep. Museums, however, often have a **taxidermy** specimen on display so you can see what the shark looks like close up. Other museums have used fossils and videos to make mechanical versions of these deepwater sharks.

## VOLUNTEER

Aquariums often have many different shark species, and they are always looking for people who are willing to volunteer to help out in some way, such as cleaning or showing visitors around. You can learn about all the different kinds of sea life on display, and may even get a chance to help with feeding a shark. You won't be able to see some of the deepest sea dwellers at an aquarium, but it will help you learn about the kinds of life that oceans hold.

Volunteering at an aquarium is one way to learn more about the ocean.

## BECOME AN OCEANOGRAPHER

If you want to learn more about sharks and the ocean, you may want to become an oceanographer. You will encounter many kinds of ocean life, both plants and animals, and you will learn how things like underground volcanoes work, and what happens when there is an earthquake in the ocean. Oceanographers are the scientists most responsible for helping us protect both the oceans and the land that is affected by oceanic events.

You could become an oceanographer like these scientists who are launching an Autonomous underwater unmanned vehicle.

## BECOME A MARINE BIOLOGIST

If the whole ocean isn't as interesting to you as the animals and plants that live there are, you might prefer to become a marine biologist. You can work in places like an aquarium, a research lab, or with a crew that travels around the world and goes deep into the sea to take pictures and learn what they can about ocean life. You can learn how to put monitors on sharks to help scientists follow them. This helps them learn about their habits, how long they live, and where they travel. Maybe you can go down in a submarine or even invent new equipment that will help other scientists learn more.

Alvin enables scientists to travel down to 14,764 ft. (4,500 m).



### MEET ALVIN

Alvin is a submersible, or submarine, that allows three people at a time to go down into the ocean to see what is happening. This easy-to-operate submarine is steered with a joystick, like you use to play video games. Windows allow the scientists to look out into the water when there is enough light, and there are several cameras attached to Alvin. Most of the cameras are video cameras, but there is also a still camera. Alvin is able to stay underwater for up to four hours at a time, but then has to come back up so the humans inside can get more air. Alvin was actually created by a scientist who wanted to go down and explore the sunken Titanic. This shows how something that is created for one purpose can end up benefiting us in a completely different way. So far, Alvin has been on more adventures than most humans!

## DEEP SEA PHOTOGRAPHY

There are a few divers who have made it their lives' work to go on diving
expeditions to photograph the life beneath the water. Underwater photography
is something that you can start learning now. Find an underwater camera,
and start at a local beach. As you learn to take good pictures underwater, you
might find yourself learning to snorkel and then dive. Over time, your skills
can become better and you can go deeper underwater and stay longer. By the
time you become an adult, you just might get a picture of some of the rarest

sharks in the ocean. Do an internet search for "underwater photographer," and you will find a lot of listings. Try going to some of the scientific sites listed, and you will really become interested in learning how they get these wonderful pictures.

## JOIN AN EXPEDITION

There still isn't enough technology for whole diving expeditions to go into the deepest parts of the ocean. However, some places offer groups of divers a chance to go down in large cages to areas where they can encounter sharks, like the great white and others that swim at a shallower level. Several of the deepwater sharks will come up into the water at this depth during the day looking for food, and it is possible you will get a chance to see them at that time. It is important when you go on these expeditions that you follow the rules. Most sharks will not attack unless they are feeling threatened, and even then, they will often do a kind of dance that lets humans know they are feeling threatened. If you learn to recognize the signs, you can often prevent an attack. Before joining one of these underwater adventures, do your homework and learn as much as you can about the kinds of sharks you may encounter.

## UNDERWATER HOTELS

Across the world, there are several places that have underwater hotels and restaurants. These don't go into the deepest parts of the ocean, but they do go far enough down where you are likely to see sharks of many kinds. If you are lucky, you may be able to see a deep-sea shark that has wandered upwards in search of prey or even out of curiosity. Sharks are often curious creatures—they find people as interesting as people find them. In their world, you are the strange one!

There are even underwater restaurants where you can dine while watching ocean creatures.

## ACCIDENTAL ENCOUNTERS

Anywhere the ocean meets land, there is a slight chance that a deepwater shark may find its way to land. In these cases, it is important to keep in mind that the shark is most likely scared and possibly ill. You can observe, but you also need to find help to get the shark back into the water so it has a chance at survival. Never harass or bother any sea animal that washes up onto the beach. Remember that they are scared and out of place and only want to go back to where they are familiar. They are even more scared of you than you are of them.

## READ

One of the best ways to get to know and understand deepwater sharks is to read everything you can about them. Try finding books by explorers who have traveled to the ocean depths, and use your imagination to put yourself in their place. Visit websites, read magazines and newspapers, and learn all you can. Start with the list at the end of this book—most of the resources will have a list of other books and articles you can explore.

## OKEANOS EXPLORER

The best way to discover what lies beneath the ocean is to spend as much time as possible researching. On August 8, 2008, the government funded a ship named the *Okeanos Explorer*. This ship's sole purpose is to sail the oceans and explore all aspects of ocean life, from the nature of tides to the living organisms that call the oceans home. Many of the scientists who are learning from her adventures (ships are always referred to as her or she) are stationed on outposts around the world and get their information through satellite. Not only scientists are able to benefit from what this ship discovers. The crew has sent video to classrooms, news stations, and many other places to help us begin to understand the almost 95 percent of the oceans we still know very little about. The *Okeanos Explorer* even has its own YouTube channel so you can see what they discover.

On board the *Okeanos Explorer*, the remotely-operated vehicle *Deep Discoverer* is being prepared for its next mission.

Some deepwater sharks, like this striped dogfish, get washed up on shore.

# CREATE YOUR OWN DEEP-SEA ENVIRONMENT

Try putting together a model of the deep-sea environment you have learned about. Find an old glass aquarium and gather some craft supplies. Learn about the environment deepwater sharks live in, and try to create that environment in your aquarium. Add sea plants to your model and create environments that mimic the real one. The more you learn, the more lifelike your environment will be. Try making this an ongoing project by adding shark models, artificial reefs, different lighting, and more. Sometimes when you have something in front of you to work with, ideas start entering your mind that help you make connections and come up with answers to questions.

Sometimes the only way to experience deepwater sharks is through art, like this megamouth shark model from Toba Aquarium in Japan.

## FINAL THOUGHTS

Every day we learn a little more about the wonderful world around us. By continually studying, you give yourself the opportunity to one day be part of a society that understands the deepest oceans as well as the world you see around you. What started out as a wish to understand this wonderfully different environment that takes up a large portion of our world, has resulted in the creation of submarines, ships, and underwater cameras. One day, this wish may grow into a way to swim with these sharks in their own environment. Who knows, maybe your great-grandchildren will find a way to actually live their lives beneath the ocean's waters in underwater cities!

The deepest part of the ocean doesn't see this much light and is over 36,000 ft. (10,973 m) deep.

## TEXT-DEPENDENT QUESTIONS:

1. What percentage of the ocean remains unexplored?

2. What do we call people who study ocean life?

3. Do sharks attack without warning?

## RESEARCH PROJECT:

There are four main ways scientists can explore the ocean floor. Do a search to find out what these four ways are, and write a brief description of how each method works. Which one of the four methods do you think would be the most exciting to use? Can you use your imagination to think up other ways that might be used in the future?

# SERIES GLOSSARY OF KEY TERMS

**Apparatus:** A device or a collection of tools that are used for a specific purpose. A diving apparatus helps you breathe under water.

**Barbaric:** Something that is considered unrefined or uncivilized. The idea of killing sharks just for their fins can be seen as barbaric.

**Buoyant:** Having the ability to float. Not all sharks are buoyant. They need to swim to stay afloat.

**Camouflage:** To conceal or hide something. Sharks' coloring often helps camouflage them from their prey.

**Chum:** A collection of fish guts and fish remains thrown into the ocean to attract sharks. Divers will often use chum to help attract sharks.

**Conservation:** The act of preserving or keeping things safe. Conservation is important in keeping sharks and oceans safe from humans.

**Decline:** To slope down or to decrease in number. Shark populations are on the decline due to human activity.

**Delicacy:** Something, particularly something to eat, that is very special and rare. Shark fin soup is seen as a delicacy in some Asian countries, but it causes a decline in shark populations.

**Expedition:** A type of adventure that involves travel for a specific purpose. Traveling to a location specifically to see sharks would be considered an expedition.

**Ferocious:** Describes something that is mean, fierce, or extreme. Sharks often look ferocious because of their teeth and the way they attack their prey.

**Finning:** The act of cutting off the top (dorsal) fin of a shark specifically to sell for meat. Sharks cannot swim without all of their fins, so finning leads to a shark's death.

**Frequent:** To go somewhere often. Sharks tend to frequent places where there are lots of fish.

**Ft.:** An abbreviation for feet or foot, which is a unit of measurement. It is equal to 12 inches or about .3 meters.

**Indigenous:** Native to a place or region.

**Intimidate:** To scare or cause fear. Sharks can intimidate other fish and humans because of their fierce teeth.

**Invincible:** Unable to be beaten or killed. Sharks seem to be invincible, but some species are endangered.

**KPH:** An abbreviation for kilometers per hour, which is a metric unit of measurement for speed. One kilometer is equal to approximately .62 miles.

**M:** An abbreviation for meters, which is a metric unit of measurement for distance. One meter is equal to approximately 3.28 feet.

**Mi.:** An abbreviation for miles, which is a unit of measurement for distance. One mile is equal to approximately 1.61 kilometers.

**Migrate:** To move from one place to another. Sharks often migrate from cool to warm water for several different reasons.

**MPH:** An abbreviation for miles per hour, which is a unit of measurement for speed. One mile is equal to approximately 1.61 kilometers.

**Phenomenon:** Something that is unusual or amazing. Seeing sharks in the wild can be quite a phenomenon.

**Prey:** Animals that are hunted for food—either by humans or other animals. It can also mean the act of hunting.

**Reputable:** Something that is considered to be good or to have a good reputation. When diving with sharks, it is important to find a reputable company that has been in business for a long time.

**Staple:** Something that is important in a diet. Vegetables are staples in our diet, and fish is a staple in sharks' diets.

**Strategy:** A plan or method for achieving a goal. Different shark species have different hunting strategies.

**Temperate:** Something that is not too extreme such as water temperature. Temperate waters are not too cold or too hot.

**Tentacles:** Long arms on an animal that are used to move or sense objects. Octopi have tentacles that help them catch food.

**Vulnerable:** Something that is easily attacked. We don't think of sharks as being vulnerable, but they are when they're being hunted by humans.

## FURTHER READING

**Cerullo, Mary M.** *Sharks of the Deep: A Shark Photographer's Search for Sharks at the Bottom of the Sea.* Capstone Press (2014).

**Green, Sara.** *The Frilled Shark.* Pilot Publishing (2013). All you want to know about frilled sharks.

**Musick, John A.,** and **Beverly McMillan.** *The Shark Chronicles.* Owl Books (2003). The authors of this book gather research from shark specialists and weave that information into their own experience to create a book that tells the story of sharks in a clear and interesting style.

**Snyderman, Mary.** *Great Shark Adventures: True Tales from the Deep.* Key Porter Books (1998). Follow a deep-sea diver and her photographer friends as they tell of many adventures they've had over the years.

## INTERNET RESOURCES

**http://cnso.nova.edu**
The Halmos College of Natural Sciences and Oceanography provides shark videos and shark activity maps.

**http://cnso.nova.edu/sharktracking**
The Guy Harvey Research Institute (GHRI) Shark Tracking partners with the Halmos College of Natural Sciences and Oceanography in tracking and recording shark activity. The GHRI dedicates its resources to the preservation of marine life, including sharks.

http://saveourseas.com
The Save Our Seas Foundation specifically focuses their efforts on saving sharks and rays. Their website includes shark facts, a newsletter, and details about how to help save sharks and rays.

**http://ocean.si.edu/sharks**
This site covers all the basics on sharks, from their senses to how sharks are falsely thought to be evil predators.

**https://www.livescience.com/topics/sharks**
This site is for more advanced students who want to learn the reasons behind different shark behavior.

**http://www.nova.edu/ghoc/index.html**
Thinking of entering a career with ocean creatures, including sharks? This site offers information that can help you decide if this type of career is right for you.

**https://www.youtube.com/oceanexplorergov**
This page shows videos from the Okeanos Explorer. The ship itself is described, and the site offers copies of many of the explorations the ship has conducted.

**https://www.youtube.com/watch?v=Wh8-GTBV2-I**
Learn more about the Greenland shark, which is considered the oldest living shark species today.

# AT A GLANCE

SWIM DEPTH

200 ft.
400 ft.
600 ft.
800 ft.
1,000 ft.
1,200 ft.
1,400 ft.
1,600 ft.
1,800 ft.

Hammerhead Sharks
Length: 20 ft. (6.1 m)
Swim Depth: 262 ft. (80 m)
Lifespan: 20+ years

Bull Sharks
Length: 11.1 ft. (3.4 m)
Swim Depth: 492 ft. (150 m)
Lifespan: 18+ years

Rays
Length: 8.2 ft. (2.5 m)
Swim Depth: 656 ft. (200 m)
Lifespan: 30 years

Great White Sharks
Length: 19.6 ft. (6 m)
Swim Depth: 820 ft. (250 m)
Lifespan: 30 years

Blue Sharks
Length: 12.5 ft. (3.8 m)
Swim Depth: 1,148 ft. (350 m)
Lifespan: 20 years

Tiger Sharks
Length: 11.5 ft. (3.5 m)
Swim Depth: 1148 ft. (350 m)
Lifespan: 50 years

Thresher Sharks
Length: 18.7 ft. (5.7 m)
Swim Depth: 1200 ft. (366 m)
Lifespan: 50 years

Mako Sharks
Length: 13.1 ft. (4 m)
Swim Depth: 1,640 ft. (500 m)
Lifespan: 32 years

Source: www.iucnredlist.org

## PHOTO CREDITS



## EDUCATIONAL VIDEO LINKS

### Chapter 1
This video describes fourteen of the most unusual sharks that have been discovered so far:  http://x-qr.net/1H7w

### Chapter 2
Listen and watch as a marine biologist shows how his deepwater camera works:
http://x-qr.net/1H6B

### Chapter 3
Watch this rare video of a megamouth swimming in the ocean:
http://x-qr.net/1CzG

### Chapter 4
This video shows a "forest" from the deep ocean floor that looks like something from another planet!  http://x-qr.net/1Dd1

## AUTHOR'S BIOGRAPHY

Joyce has written nearly four-thousand articles on a multitude of subjects. She is a published book author, has answered questions at AllExperts.com, and has ghostwritten articles for over twenty-five years. She uses her forensic psychology degree to aid in writing for many fields. These fields include psychology, criminology, sales, animal behavior, color psychology, education, and psychological disorders.